D1085776

ELEGANT HERBS
&
MEDICINAL PLANTS
COLORING BOOK

Long before modern medicine and the corner drugstore, herbalists dispensed celery to treat lunacy and considered aloe a veritable wonder drug able to purify phlegm, prevent hair loss, remedy moral decay and corruption, and even rid one of stomach worms or tiny pests that crawl into the ears. Since antiquity, herbs and medicinal plants (known as simples) have been studied, documented, and used to treat a host of human complaints—physical, mental, emotional, and spiritual. Medieval medical tomes such as the twelfth-century Book of Simple Medicines, by Italian physician Matthaeus Platearius (?–1161) are appreciated today as snapshots of history.

A richly decorated French version of Platearius's book, with annotations reflecting more up-to-date medical knowledge, was created for a French royal couple in the late fifteenth century. Le Livre des simples médecines (The Book of Simple Medicines) also boasts illustrations helpful not only for species identification but also for spiritual contemplation, as alluded to in our cover image of a gallica rose and Solomon's seal: the Virgin Mary is often called the "rose without thorns," and the Latin name for Solomon's seal, inscribed on this image, is *Sigillum Sanctæ Mariæ* (seal of the Blessed Virgin).

The illustrations reproduced on this coloring book's inside covers are the work of artist Robinet Testard (fl. 1470–1523). They were selected from Le Livre des simples médecines (c. 1470), created for Louise of Savoy and her husband, Charles d'Angoulême. This vellum manuscript is in the collection of the National Library, St. Petersburg, Russia.

Pomegranate

Item No. CB201

Designed by Tristen Jackman

PRINTED IN KOREA

Pomegranate Communications, Inc.
19018 NE Portal Way, Portland OR 97230
800 227 1428   www.pomegranate.com

Pomegranate Europe
Number 3 Siskin Drive, Middlemarch Business Park
Coventry CV3 4FJ, UK
+44 (0)24 7621 4461   sales@pomegranate.com

Pomegranate's mission is to invigorate, illuminate, and inspire through art.

This product is in compliance with the CPSIA. A General Conformity Certificate and tracking information are available through Pomegranate.

27 26 25 24 23 22 21 20 19 18   10 9 8 7 6 5 4 3 2 1

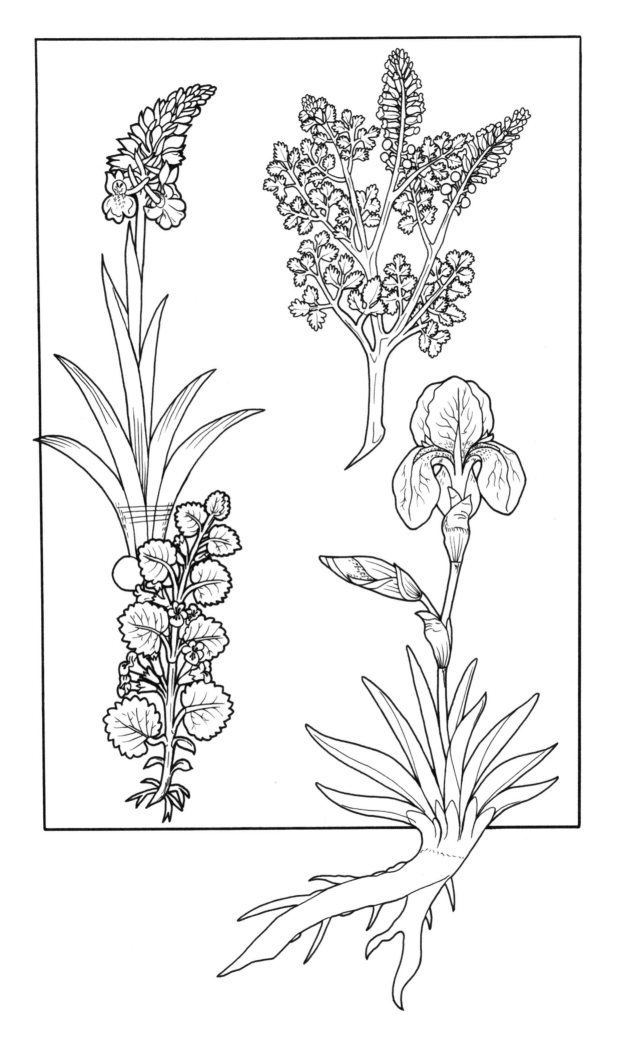

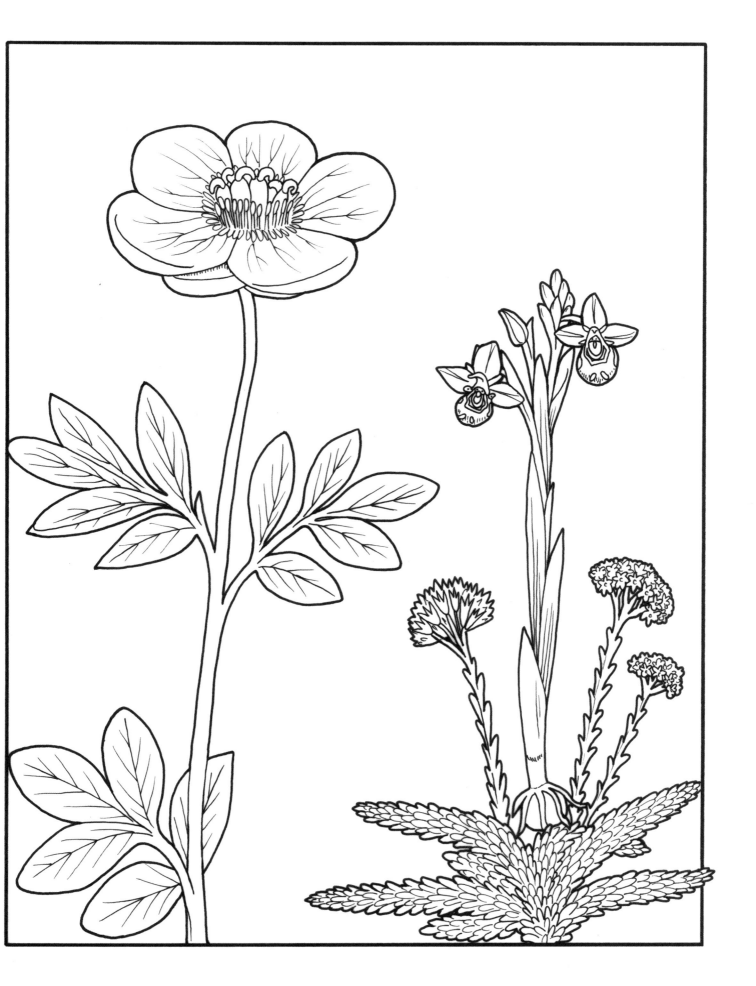

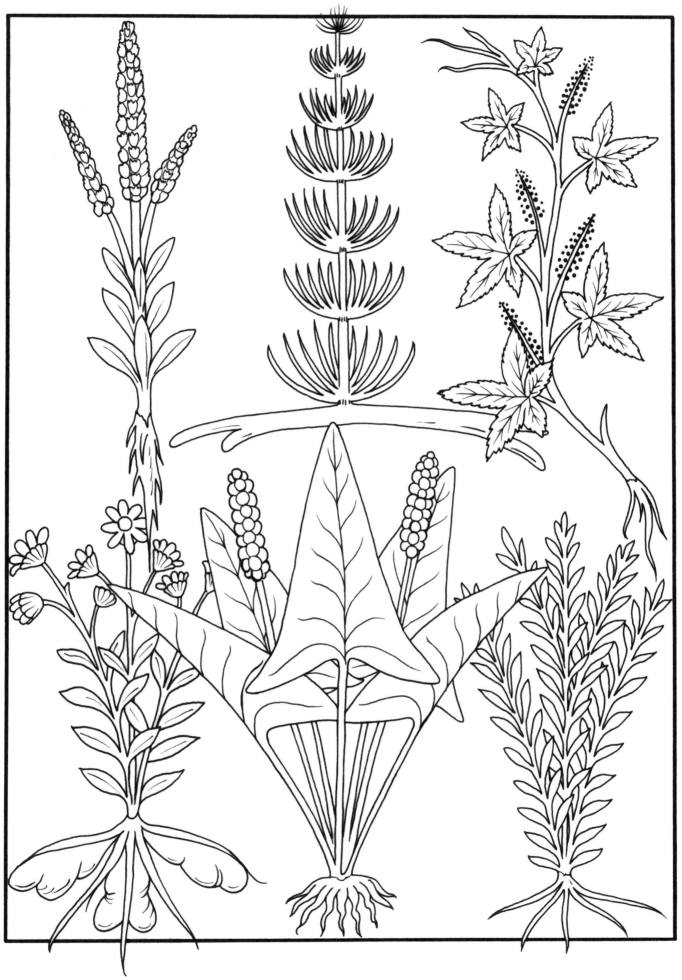

4

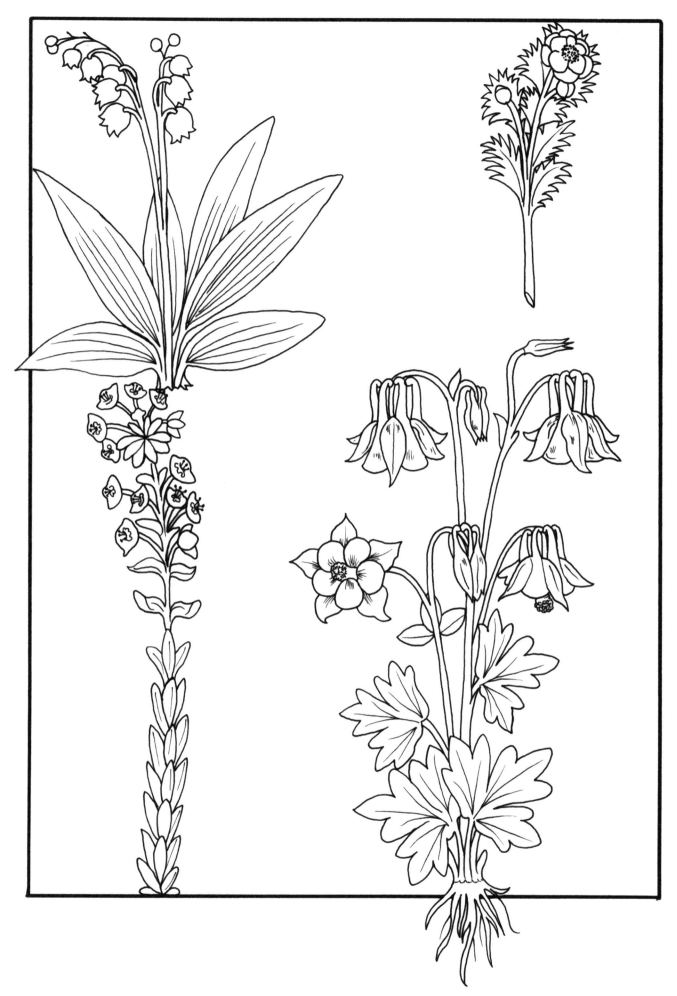

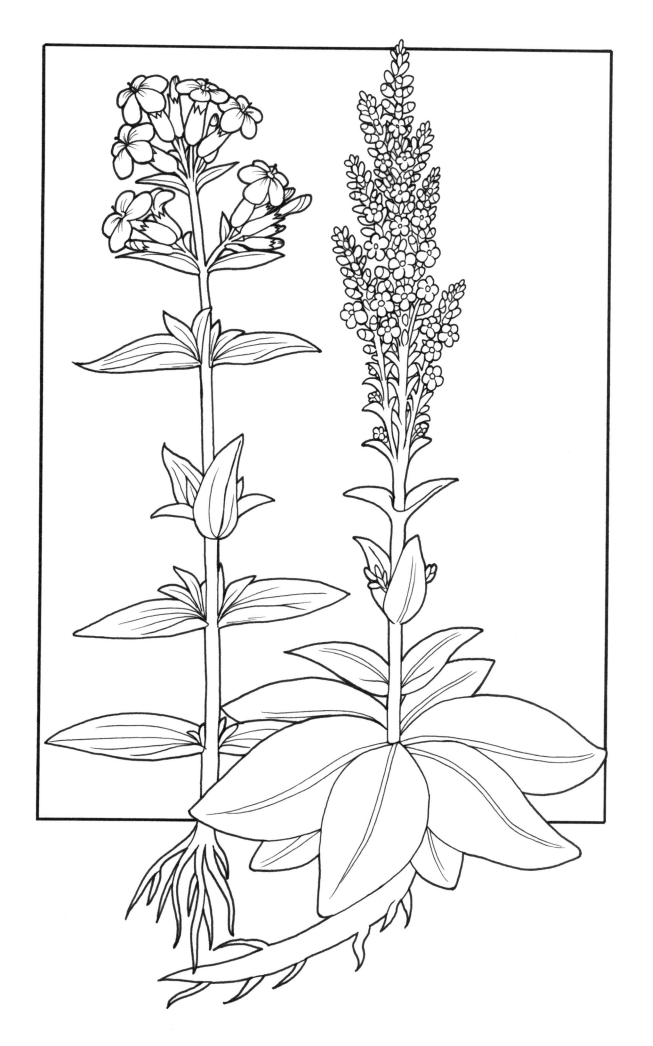

11

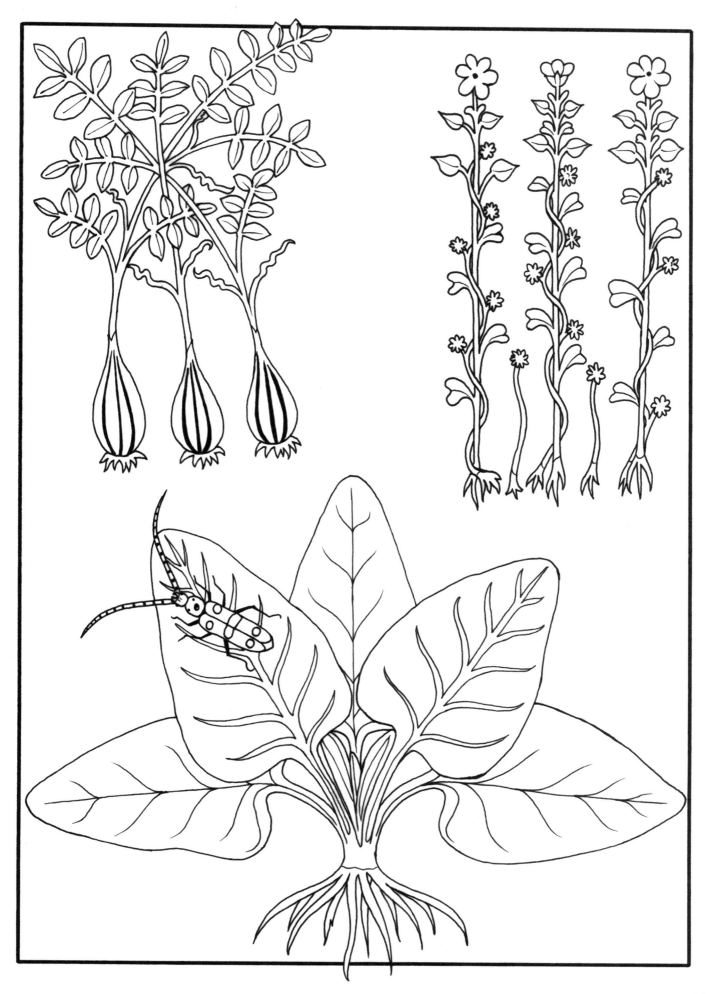

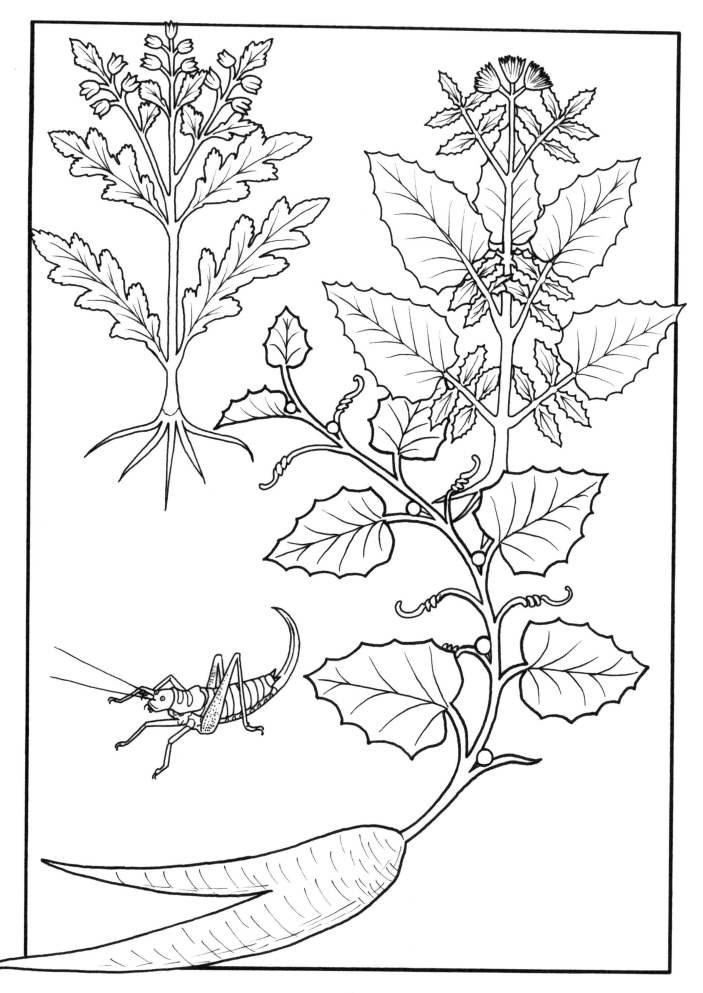

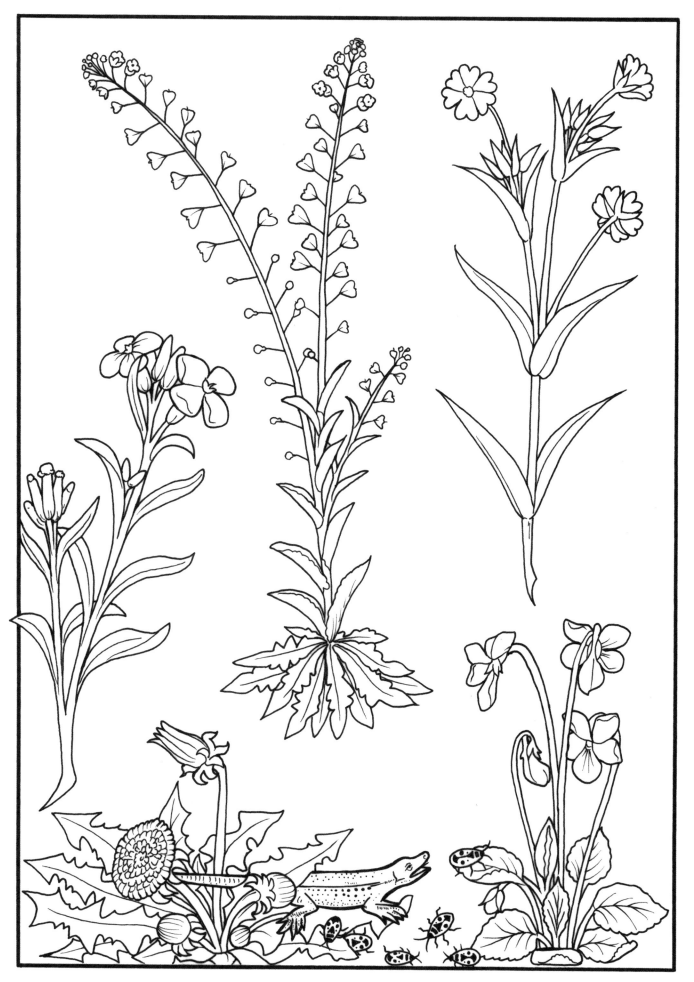

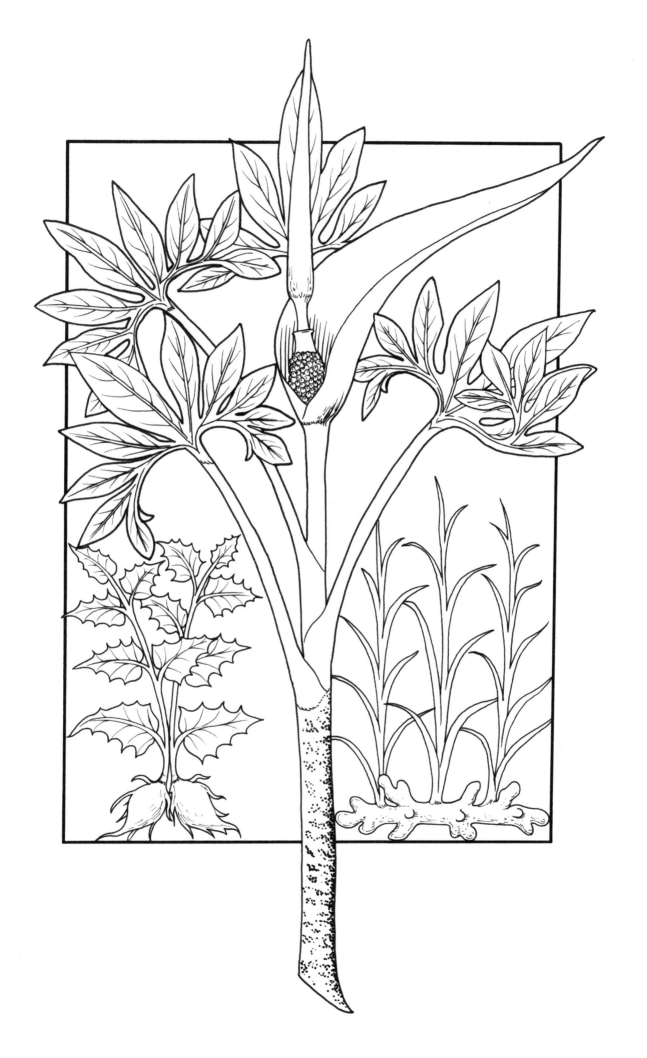

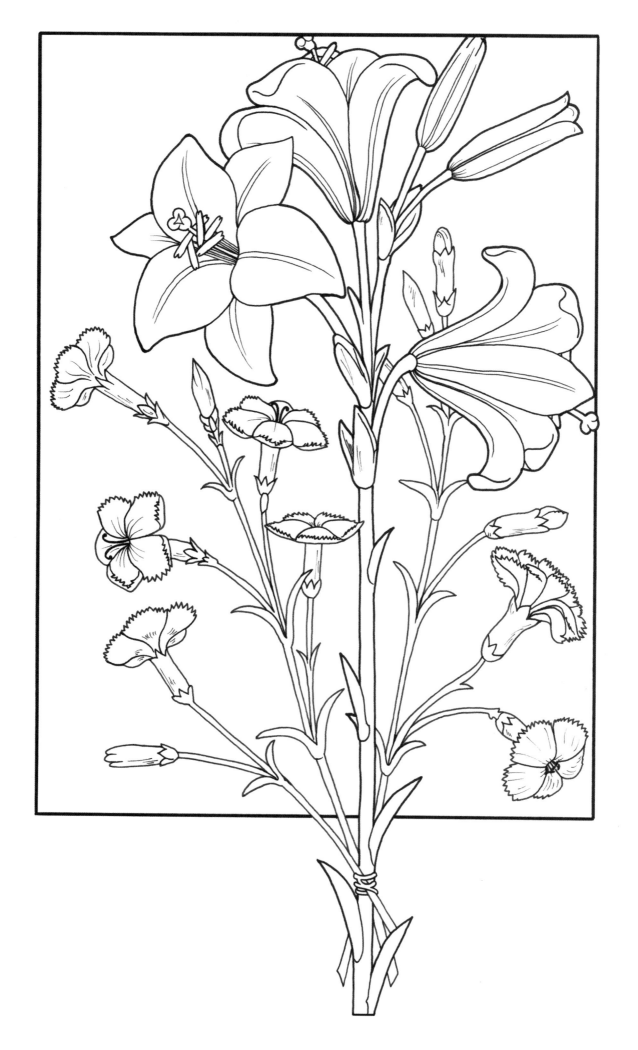

Draw and color your own picture here!